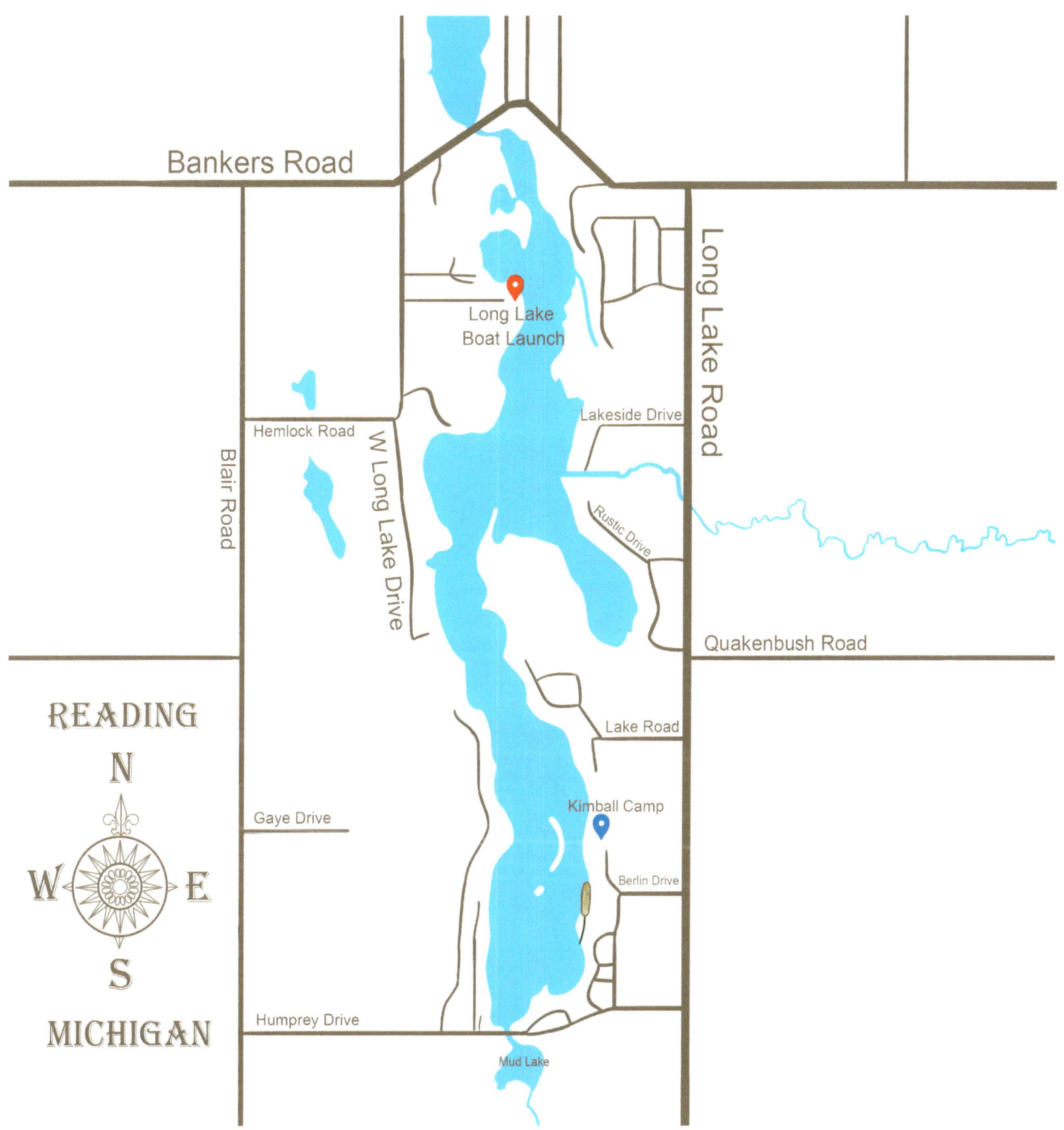

Bankers Road
Long Lake Road
Long Lake Boat Launch
Hemlock Road
Blair Road
W Long Lake Drive
Lakeside Drive
Rustic Drive
Quakenbush Road
Lake Road
Kimball Camp
Berlin Drive
READING
N
W
E
S
MICHIGAN
Gaye Drive
Humprey Drive
Mud Lake

This book is dedicated to

My wife Bonita

and my children

Caleb

Kallie

Corban

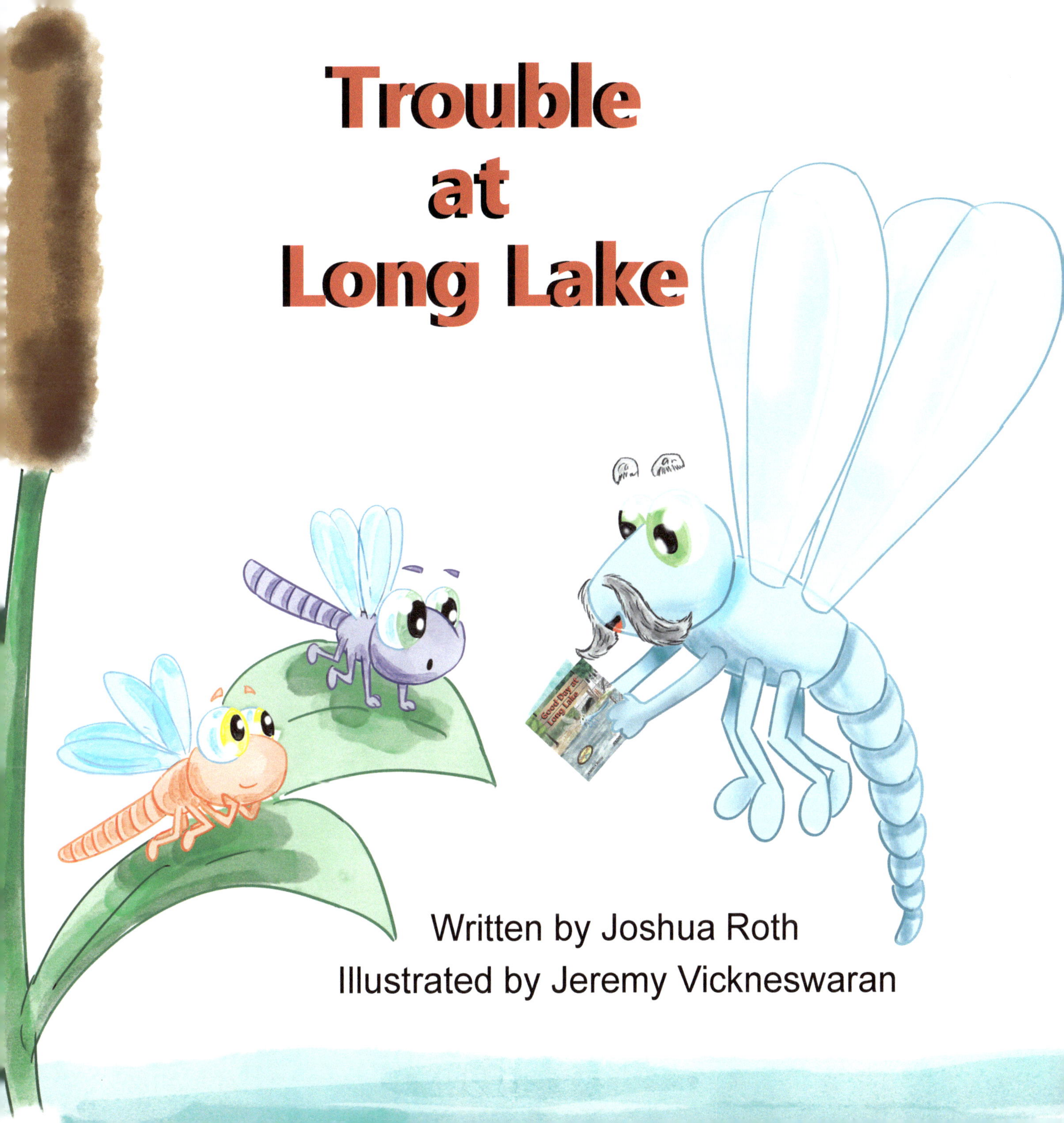

Trouble
at
Long Lake

Written by Joshua Roth
Illustrated by Jeremy Vickneswaran

Good Day at
Long Lake

Darla the dragonfly was just doing her morning mail run to Dick's cattail home when, out of the water, popped a frantic Fred the fish.

"Help!" he said. "My friend Tabitha the turtle is in trouble!"

"What on earth seems to be the problem?" asked Dick.

"It's Gary the Gar; I think he hurt Tabitha; hurry, follow me!"

Dick and Darla followed Fred towards the channel leading to Mud Lake, where they found Tabitha
upside down on a tree stump in the water.

7

"Gary is very mean and thought it was funny to put me here upside down, and now I can't turn over," said Tabitha.

Dick and Darla tried to turn Tabitha over but were not big enough to do it.

9

Dick saw a fisherman in a boat near the lily pads and got an idea.

Dick flew over to the boat
and started buzzing around the fisherman's head.

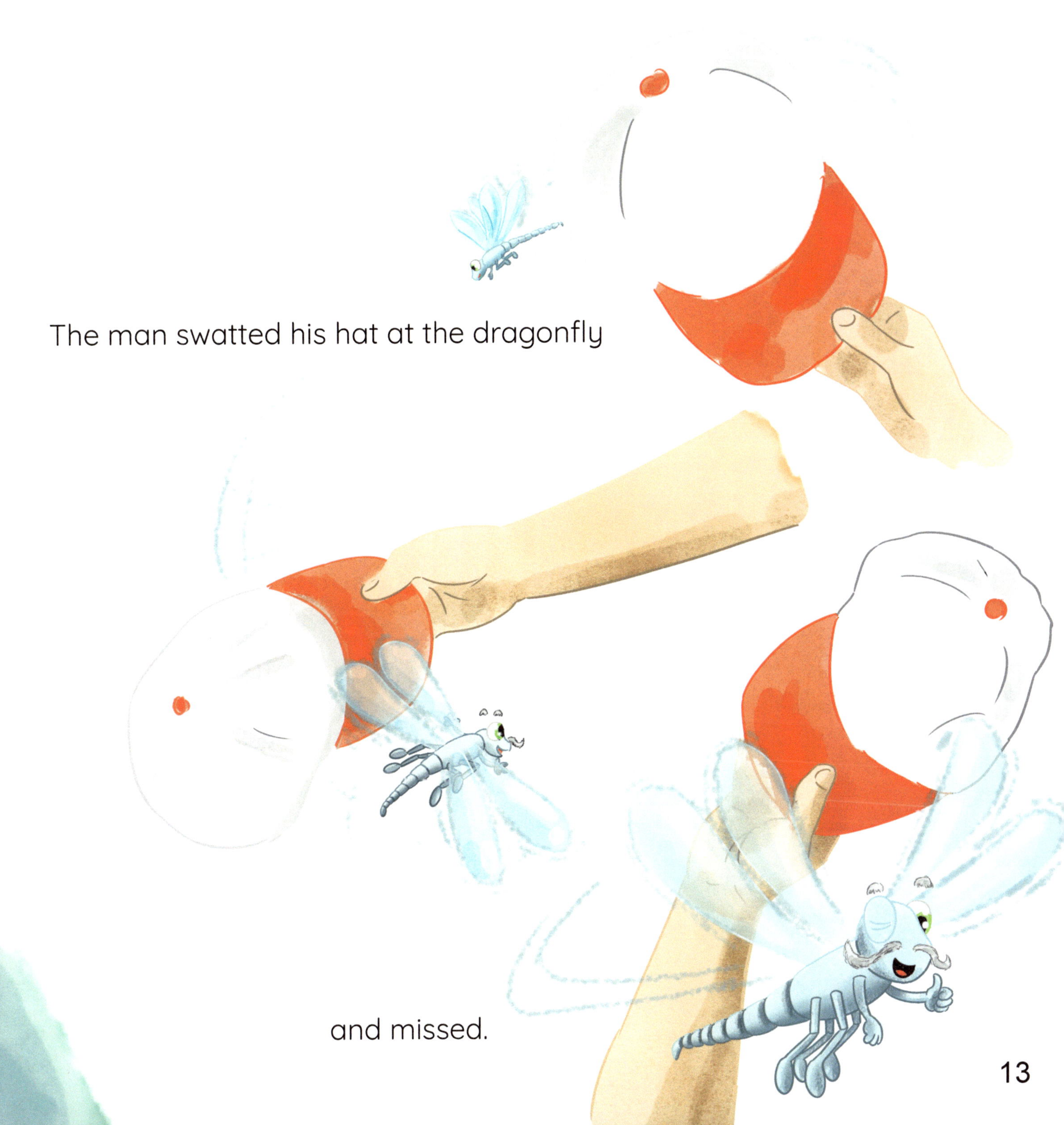

The man swatted his hat at the dragonfly

and missed.

Then Dick dropped down into the open tackle box and picked up a bright yellow and orange bobber.

Dick held the bobber in front of the confused fisherman's face

and then flew back to Tabitha and dropped the bobber straight down into the water next to the stump.

The fisherman started his boat motor
and drove over to the stump,

where he saw the upside-down painted turtle
kicking her legs in distress.

He turned off his motor, gently reached down,
and picked up the turtle.

As the fisherman held the turtle in front of his face, he believed he saw the pretty turtle smiling.

The fisherman then placed Tabitha into the water

as he retrieved his bobber

and then slowly drove away.

Tabitha was very thankful for Fred and the quick thinking of his friend Dick.

"Now the question is, what do we do about Gary the bully?" said Dick.

"I don't know about you, but Gary scares me with those big teeth. Just a few days ago, he chased my entire school of bluegills all over the north end of the lake," said Fred.

21

Tabitha then said, "Just yesterday I saw him come up out of the water behind a frog that was just sunbathing on a lily pad and swatted him into the lake with his big tail.

"Well," said Dick, "it sounds to me like we need to find a way to stop Gary from causing so much trouble around the lake."

"I have an idea!"
said Tabitha.
"Just last week,
the children from the big white
cottage on the hill came out to
the channel in their row boat."

"They caught me in a net and took me back with them."

"Then what did
they do?" asked
Dick.

"They played
with me for a
little while

and then put me back in
the water," replied Tabitha.

"I don't think we are going to catch Gary in a net, but maybe there is a way we can do something nice for him that makes him want to be our friend." said Dick.

Darla spoke up, "Everyone likes to get packages in the mail because it is like a gift and always a surprise to open when it arrives. Maybe there is something we can give to him."

Dick replied, "I think I know the perfect thing we can do for Gary. Let's invite him to a party in his honor."

So the group went to work decorating the shoreline around his cattail home,

and he was even able to find a couple left-over pop streamers from the Fourth of July.

Later in the evening, it was Fred's job to go and invite Gary to the party. Fred was a little unsure and scared of what Gary might do, but Dick assured him that everything would be okay.

Fred found Gary swimming near the pier at the public boat landing. Nervously, Fred said,"Uh, Mister Gary, sir?".
Long Lake
PUBLIC ACCESS
MICHIGAN DNR
Gary replied with a growl, "What do you want?"
"We would like to invite you to a party at Dick's cattail home."

Gary was a little surprised at the request and decided to follow Fred to the party. When they arrived, everyone yelled, "Surprise!!".

The pop streamers flew through the air, and everyone clapped.

Dick then stood at the doorway of his home and said, "Congratulations! We have nominated you, Gary, as the Guardian of all fish, turtles, frogs, and wildlife in the lake. We would like to present you with this badge of honor and make you our new friend."

With a tear in his eye, Gary said, "No one has ever wanted to be my friend and throw me a party before, and I would like very much for you to be my friends."

With everyone gone for the night, Dick crawled into bed and smiled at the thought of their new friend Gary the Gar proudly taking on the task of Guardian of the lake.